Safe Kids
Safety on the Go

Dana Meachen Rau

Marshall Cavendish
Benchmark
New York

Ready to go?

You can ride in a bus,
in a car, or on a bike!

Wait for the bus on the sidewalk.

Do not step into the street.

Walk carefully up and down the steps.

You would not want to fall.

The bus driver needs to watch the road.

Stay in your seat and do not shout.

Stay in your seat in a car, too.

Sit in the back in a *booster seat*.

Put on your seat belt.

Make sure you hear
it click.

Do not put your hands out the window.

Keep the doors locked.

Be safe when you ride a bike, too.

Ask an adult if you can go.

Always wear a *helmet*.

Helmets protect your head if you fall.

Cars move fast.

Look both ways before crossing.

Keep your eyes on
the road.

You could fall if you hit
a rock or a hole.

Keep both hands on your bike.

Keep both wheels on the ground.

Be a safe kid on the go.

Be Safe

bike

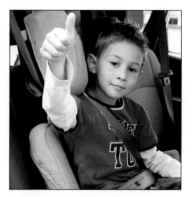

booster seat

helmets

hole

seat belts

sidewalk

Challenge Words

booster seat A special seat to make you taller in the car.

helmet (HEL-muht) A hard covering that protects your head.

Index

Page numbers in **boldface** are illustrations.

About the Author

Dana Meachen Rau is the author of many other titles in the Bookworms series, as well as other nonfiction and early reader books. She lives in Burlington, Connecticut, with her husband and two children.

With thanks to the Reading Consultants:

Nanci Vargus, Ed.D., is an Assistant Professor of Elementary Education at the University of Indianapolis.

Beth Walker Gambro is an Adjunct Professor at the University of Saint Francis in Joliet, Illinois.

Marshall Cavendish Benchmark
99 White Plains Road
Tarrytown, New York 10591-9001
www.marshallcavendish.us

Library of Congress Cataloging-in-Publication Data

Rau, Dana Meachen, 1971-
Safety on the go / by Dana Meachen Rau.
p. cm. — (Bookworms: Safe kids)
Includes index.
Summary: "Identifies common transportation hazards and advises how to deal with them"
—Provided by publisher.
ISBN 978-0-7614-4085-7
1. Transportation—Safety measures—Juvenile literature. 2. Traffic
safety—Juvenile literature. I. Title.
HE194.R38 2010
613.6'8—dc22
2008044932

Editor: Christina Gardeski
Publisher: Michelle Bisson
Designer: Virginia Pope
Art Director: Anahid Hamparian

Photo Research by Anne Burns Images

Cover Photo by *SuperStock*/UpperCut Images

The photographs in this book are used with permission and through the courtesy of:
Getty Images: pp. 1, 17 Jenny Acheson; p. 3 Matt Henry Gunther; pp. 5, 29R Dave Nagel;
pp. 7 David Young-Wolf; p. 9 Siri Stafford; p. 15 SW Productions. *Alamy Images*: pp. 11, 21, 28TR
INSADCO Photography; pp. 25, 28TL Picture Partners. *Photo Edit*: pp. 13, 23, 28BR, 29L David
Young Wolf. *SuperStock*: pp. 19, 28BL age fotostock. *Corbis*: p. 27 Kelly-Mooney Photography.

Printed in Malaysia
1 3 5 6 4 2